Unconscious Memories

Volume 1

Up To The Dreamer

Kristen Andersen

BALBOA.PRESS
A DIVISION OF HAY HOUSE

Balboa Press books may be ordered through booksellers or by contacting:

Balboa Press
A Division of Hay House
1663 Liberty Drive
Bloomington, IN 47403
www.balboapress.com
1 (877) 407-4847

Print information available on the last page.

ISBN: 978-1-9822-4444-6 (sc)
ISBN: 978-1-9822-4446-0 (hc)
ISBN: 978-1-9822-4445-3 (e)

Library of Congress Control Number: 2020904728

Balboa Press rev. date: 03/09/2020

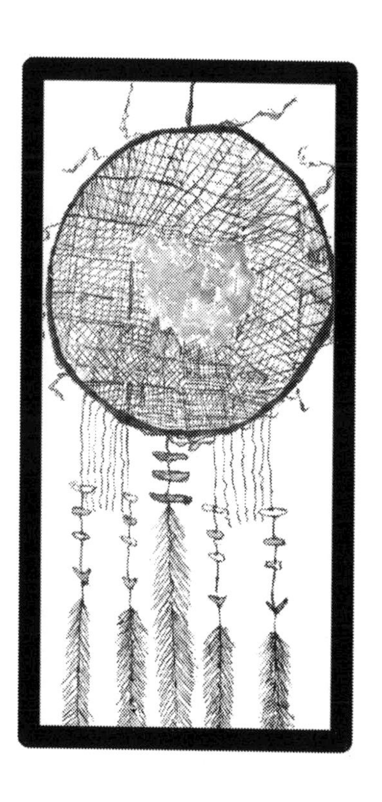

Table of Contents

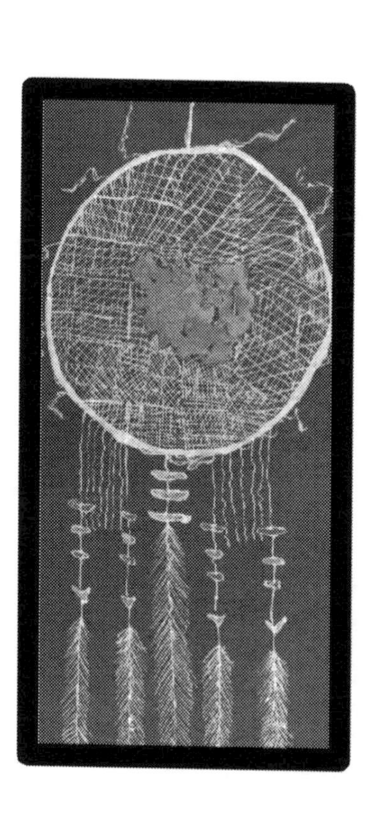

Introduction

I want you to know that I am not a researcher of dreams. I am not an expert about the unconscious mind. I am also not an interpreter of your dream experiences or knowledgeable about your associated emotions. I am however, longing to share what I have learned from these incredible and personal stories rooted in the depths of my mind. Through dream experiences, I have learned that when I am honest with myself, I can accurately interpret and understand the meaning to assist my waking life. I have learned that only I can determine the authentic relevance of my dreams. I have learned so much about the inner workings of myself, all by going to sleep.

So, maybe you had a dream last night, last month or last year. Maybe you think dreams are insightful, entertainment or therapeutic. Maybe you think dreams are irrelevant or nonsense. Maybe none of these. No matter if you vividly remember or what you think about dreaming, hopefully my sharing of these intense narratives will inspire you to interpret your own dreams by being honest with yourself and in turn, assist your waking life. The activity of the unconscious mind while we sleep, is a fascinating unknown. A mind that unconsciously creates stories to be stored as part of a conscious memory is simply, incredible.

So, I write to you with no concrete interpretation, but only having experienced dreams as vast as pure love, as awkward as bizarre sex, and as deep as the yearning for connection. I write to you from a mind haunted by stories of hardship, pain, and unimaginable demons. I write to you extraordinarily fulfilled by the wonder and stunning beauty of impossible environments and enlightening revelations. I write to you from unconscious places where animals speak, and the ability to perform illogical acts without consequence is natural. I write to you vulnerable and amazed. I write to you bewildered and fascinated by the world of dreams. With great humility, gratitude, and detail, I share my unconscious mind with you. I write to you from my unconscious memories.

AT
THE
THEATER

At The Theater

You go to the movies with your love and walk into the dark theater while holding hands. You sit down with the one you love in a row with a lot of people. You are both so exhausted from the day. As you watch the movie of no immediate significance, you both start to fall asleep. Your love stretches out their body and leans to the left where they are on top of other people in your theater row. The people next to you in your row are upset with you both but, at the same time, they are laughing about how silly and ridiculous both of you are. They were continuing to get angry while laughing at how you were falling all over them, showing signs of dizziness while half-sleeping through the movie. Secretly, you both attempt to fool around in a dark theater thinking no one can see you. You both feel so daring.

The people next to you finally get up and leave. You and your love attempt to move down to the end of the row, but more people show up and take the empty seats. You suddenly get an urge to use the restroom. When you get up from your chair, you are extremely dizzy and feel like you are going to pass out. You are so faint that you decide to crawl the rest of your way upon the dirty, sticky, sugary, popcorn polluted theater floor. Suddenly you notice a tall, dark, and handsome fellow who is following you to the bathroom. You find him attractive but creepy, and you know for certain there is something wrong with him and his intentions. His presence is making you feel very uncomfortable.

You are frightened, and you feel like you are in danger. You think about rape and being beaten. You foresee all the pain and injustice unleashed on your mind, body, and soul. Your fear escalates. You are terrified as the handsomely creepy man gets closer and closer to you. You maneuver yourself through the mazelike restroom to lose the man who you know will hurt you. You are unable to relieve yourself in the bathroom because you are much too afraid. You are so caught up in escaping the man that you can't even urinate. You are disappointed and in pain.

Still feeling dizzy, you do not want to fall. You decide to crawl again, only this time you make your way on your hands and knees through the restroom of piss, shit, shoe tracks, and polluted toilet paper. You see the same man outside of the restroom as you stand up from the filth and scream a frightful shriek. You are so terrified that you let out a holler so loud, so violent, so intense that it shatters the glass theater windows. You are still so dizzy, scared, and unhinged by your terror of being violated by the mysteriously odd and handsome man. You think to yourself, why did I ever leave my theater seat?

The man who had been following you the entire time makes it seem like you are crazy and that he was never following you at all. The man walks away from you and sits in the theater's diner booth to eat with a group of 8 male friends. You follow him and tell him how much he terrified you and, he doesn't care. He laughs at you. You begin to believe you are wrong and apologize to him for mistaking his intentions. He violently snickers at you.

You realize again that you are the one who is wrong. You embrace the falsities of your character by apologizing again and, he finally and gratefully accepts.

Throughout the conversation with the man and now after, you remain unsteady and lightheaded to where you feel you are going to pass out again. You struggle a bit to get your balance but, you finally do after a few moments of palpitating panic. You reenter the theater to find your love. As you re-enter the dark theater, you see your lover with an elf-looking, thin, blonde, and beautifully complexed white female. The woman is on top of your love, your partner, your life. You hope that what you are seeing is incorrect. You watch them make out and touch each other all over. You stand there hoping they stop and see you in the dark, but they do not. The remaining people in the row watching the film are making sounds of, "oh" and "awe" as they recognize you watching the deceit and unfaithfulness unveil before your eyes.

Your love looks up at you, finally recognizing you are there, and gives you an indescribable face of shame, shock, and arrogance. The woman looks up as well and smiles at you in a very peculiar and devious way. A tear runs down your face and, you feel empty inside. The people in the row chime in again and say to you "What are you crying about? You really thought you were the only one?" They snicker through their commentary and, you feel the crushing pain of betrayal. You hope that your love will stop while you experience the deepest of heartbreaks but, when you look back over, nothing changes and, the unfaithful deception continues without shame. You have enough watching. You have enough waiting. You begin to walk out of the dark theater and, you think to yourself, what a waste of time and say out loud, "Well, it is 4:41 am, just about time to wake up." And now, it's just another memory.

DRAGON EYE

Dragon Eye

The dragon is huge and chasing you up the chimney. It is tricking you with its every move. She is there again, your partner in crime and best friend from elementary school. There you both are together, up in an attic of a three-story house looking out on the deeply blackened night sky. You and she couldn't have been a better team. You are both in complete sync. Like two condors scraping the stars with pointed-cutting wings just lunging and plowing with grace and style. "We got this", you think to yourself. You both creep in and out of every room of the house. You sneak and work hard to escape the giant winged beast.

There is not much else for you and her to do but learn how to evade and kill the dragon. You both dredge through the mansion to hide behind any wall you can find. Unluckily, you are close to an attic window where the dragon peaks its eye and sees you both. After being spotted, you run to the floating dock connected to the mansion and hide behind barrels full of water. You speak in quiet tones and whispers to devise your next moves. You both converse so near. You are so close that you can see the yellow in her hair, the freckles on her cheeks and nose, and the sparkles in her big blue eyes.

She is your dearest friend and always will be. You know that so much of what you are, is also part of her. You know the two of you have what it takes to make it through the challenge, the fear, the physical fight. As you gaze at her and breathe heavily through your thoughts on what to do next, you suddenly see a silhouette of a man. The man you see is your brother! "Bro, what are you doing here!?!?", You speak with a tone of joy and a huge smile on your face. He smiles back and replies with intensity, "I am here because we have got to stick together and get rid of the dragon!"

He begins to help you and your friend climb up shafts of the mansion out of the path of the beast. You work together to glide up the pinnacles of the structure. He is there to help and rescue and, it is what you have always wanted. You want him to save you and, you have all the confidence that he will. He is your big brother. He is fearless. He is agile. He is your blood. He is a savior. There is nothing he cannot do. After the three of you make your way up and down the scales of the mountain style building, all of you come upon a river moat where the dragon quickly crashes and drags its claws deep into the water and down into the sand. Your brother stares the beast directly in the eye and, you have his back if anything happens. You look around and, your elementary school friend disappears. Now, it is just you and your brother left to tackle the wild scaly creature.

You both plunge in and out of the water dodging the dragon side to side. You see your brother draw a sword and wave it in the air. Your sibling is unafraid. He is un-phased. He is skilled and determined. He is the definition of brilliant. After a few stellar moves, he shines the chrome of his sword against the light of the moon and reflects it into the dragon's eye. You run under the bridge of the moat, like something in a video game you once played together as children. You wait and watch your brother as he confuses and manipulates the dragon to distract it from destroying the mansion and everyone in it. He precisely knows what he is doing, and you have all the confidence in him. He is ultimately, a hero.

"Well done brother", is all you can think in your mind, "Well done." However, your brother isn't finished yet, he continues to work the dragon's wings hard. He tires the beast and slips away under the bridge of the moat for safety. Your brother is right next to you. You speak a few words to one another, but at the volume of a whisper. Neither of you fully hear what you or he are saying. You keep quiet, low, and safe. Your brother looks up at the dragon, you look at your brother, and your elementary school friend reappears safely. You feel some reassurance in the fate of your lives but, you know deep inside the battle carries on. And now, it's just another memory.

EMPTY
YOUR
POCKETS

Empty Your Pockets

You are with your best friend from elementary school. She shows up a lot these days. You see her consistently and without fail. You are both spies and have this hotel room for cover. You sneak around to collect information although you are uncertain what type of information you are looking for. You work at the intelligence agency together and as far as you both know you have been sent on this mission for a good reason. You look to the floor of the hotel room and see it is flooded with papers and gadgets. You attempt to keep searching for information but hear a noise. Suddenly, you are dangling outside the hotel room window. You are attached by a bungee cord and some other loose rope. You try to get back in the room but, the weight of your body and your pockets are too heavy for you to swing yourself inside.

You look down and around, and see you are dangling at least 1,000 feet in the air. You check underneath and see majestic mountain ranges. You are excitingly short of breath. The steepness and depth are incredible. You continue to dangle outside the hotel window and try to come up with a solution to get back inside. All around you are fierce and forceful winds. Directly behind you is the bluest ocean you have ever seen. You feel a cold breeze and rapid wind strongly against your face. You find the scenery overwhelmingly beautiful but the heights incredibly terrifying. You hang onto this fragile connection as you stare into beauty while suspended in air.

You look down at the bungee and rope and see that your elementary school friend is attached to you. You continue to sway in mid-air from extreme gusts of wind. She is curled up beneath you and, connected by the rope. You do all the hard work to stay alive and, she feels like deadweight. You know the bungee and rope will not hold the both of you for long. You must get back inside the window. The wind gushes again and again as you try to conjure a plan. You have several essential items in your pockets but, you are unsure what they are. You do not want to make any sudden moves, so nothing will fall out. You are managing but struggling to get into the window. The freezing wind and visual distractions of the mountain range slow you down. You are under the bluest sky and brightest sun. You throw your weight toward the window and, slowly crack it open. Cranking, thrusting and pushing, you are making headway. You continue to push, crank, and crack the window!

You sense something to your left and feel the presence of a cleaning man on a scaffold moving in your direction. You do not see him, you sense him. You perceive him coming forward while you dangle from the high rise. Your deadweight of an elementary school friend isn't moving. You know that you must hurry but can only move so quickly against the elements and your overfilled pockets. You must get back in the window before the cleaning man on the scaffold discovers you both. More importantly, you must hurry back into the window before you lose your grip and potentially fall 1,000 feet below. For a minute, your elementary school friend loses consciousness from fear. She is curled up into a ball just underneath the hotel windowsill where she appears protected and still attached to your rope. She is in the fetal position and unconscious. You look at her and know she is still not awake or moving. You begin to worry and panic.

You are closer to the window and try again to push it open. This time, you use all your limbs. You leave your friend where she is safe, so nothing will happen to her. You continue to pry open the window, and know you have very little time left. You try and try and try. You manage to widen a small slit at the bottom of the window where you can squeeze through. You know you will have to push quite intensely to fit, but you need to get back into the hotel room safely. It is a tiny window and, you know it is going to be almost impossible to make it through with everything you are carrying in your pockets. You look beneath the windowsill and, your friend is still passed out. You feel the wind ripping and roaring across your back, through your hair, and on your face. You are continuously working on the window to open it and occasionally look behind at the ocean, down at the mountain ranges and, up at the sun for reassurance.

You feel the cleaning man on the scaffold get closer and closer to discovering you both. Your elementary school friend abruptly awakens to help you. She pushes herself up on her knees to her chest and, together you shove her through the window opening. She is relieved, inside the hotel room, and cuts the rope. You feel the man on the scaffold creeping nearer. You must get yourself through the window. You are alone and dangling in mid-air. You are vulnerable but admire the beauty all around you. You know you need to empty your pockets.

You have all kinds of stuff in your pockets. All the items are important things that you do not want to lose. You start to recognize some of the items. You see your chap-stick, a lighter, and IDs. There are some other odds and ends but, the stuff is unrecognizable because of how distracted you are by the prevention of losing things. There is an intensity behind not losing anything and, you must be careful not to let anything drop. You begin to hand over and throw all your pocketed items through the crooked, cracked, and quarter of a way open, hotel room window. Your elementary school friend grabs as much as she can. You know you need to hurry and empty your pockets enough to stay alive. She is carefully grabbing everything and making sure it is all safe. You are happy the window is open and that you are saving these treasures. She is smiling but, you both are worried about your safety since you continue to dangle above the skyline. You quickly look below again at the grandest mountains you have ever seen and, the wind challenges your stability.

You are unafraid but anxious and need to get back into the window as soon as possible. The sense of urgency grows. You know the bungee is not going to hold you for much longer. You may have about 30 seconds before you fall to your death. You must get your pockets empty entirely and expeditiously to be safe. You hand off the last bit of items through the window to your friend. Finally, your pockets are empty. You are confident in not losing anything and will be able to squeeze through the hotel window to get back in. You harness yourself up by your arms. You then push yourself up using every muscle you have. You feel your strength. You know you can do it. You squeeze your entire body through the small, tight, and cracked window opening.

Once you start to climb through, it is relatively easy to get inside. You are almost all the way in. You make a last kick through the window and plunge in face first. You are finally back inside the hotel. You are both so relieved that you made it. You made it without being discovered by the cleaning man on the scaffold and before potentially falling thousands of feet. You saved your life. You saved her life. You both begin to organize all your goods that were in your pockets but, are now scattered all over the floor. You have done quite well for yourselves and, you both acknowledge the abundance and prosperity. You feel accomplished and rejoice together. You are rendered speechless with a smile. And now, it's just another memory.

goodbye moon

Goodbye Moon

You are on the surface of the Earth and, it is nighttime. You are wandering around the city and, it appears as a forest. You recognize the city as nature and giant trees. You fixate on the sky and the moon. The moon looks so huge and like it is coming toward the Earth's rotation. You feel the pull of the moon's gravity and see how everyone in the forest city is reacting. People are screaming, running, and terrified. Military officers' line the streets and encompass the natural fields. There are military trucks and helicopters circling and searching for an explanation of why the moon is so close to the Earth. The chaos is horrifying, and you feel the fear within your soul. You hate to look up even though you feel you must.

You are in shock at how the moon looks and why it is the way it is. For a moment, you do not know what you are feeling but, you can sense the pull of the atmosphere sucking on your body from the inside-out. You are unsure how anyone is handling this because of how strange and strong the pull is operating. The chaos around you grows. People fight over resources, random items, and water. You cannot believe what is happening around you. You are alone and in awe over the moons closeness and the way it is making you feel. You see the military standing by watching the subtle yet erratic changes of the moon.

You begin to wonder how things are going to pan out when you suddenly feel a shock wave against your body. You watch a portion of the moon explode into a few large chunks and the chunks then, burst into a billion pieces. Everyone who was only mildly scared before is now perpetually terrified. The city of forest is in disarray. You see shattered fragments of the moon's surface fly by you and crash to the Earth's ground. You see the remaining rock tilting to the right and getting closer to the lithosphere. You feel clueless while you watch the remainder of the moon spontaneously catch on fire. Now the moon drips hot lava and exudes coal-like wholes that glow. You are very scared. You experience your body being pulled in all different directions. You can see the fear in everyone who is trying to escape the reality of the future. You run and dodge pieces of the moon as you watch it get even closer to the Earth's surface. You feel the gravity pulling you more and more until it picks you up off the ground. The drastic change propels you to float 5-feet in the air.

Once grounded to the Earth's force, you are now a floating and vulnerable being, unable to attach yourself to any such grander energy than your own. You are unsure on what to do so you grab ahold of a large tree branch. The tree is your salvation and, you feel safe while grasping its bulked limbs. You never thought this was going to be your fate. You never thought you would see the world end this way. A few military officers see you hanging onto the tree and think you are brilliant. They believe that you have found the key to surviving the atmospheric tragedy. They never speak to you but, they telepathically ask you to be part of saving what remains of the moon. You do not decline but you do not agree.

So, you let go. You let go of the tree and simultaneously let go of the Earth.

You float up passed the spheres of Earth and drift by the fiery moon. You propel and slingshot around the fire using the force of your body. You result under a 20-foot high glass-covered dome on the other side of the moon. There are already several people there, waiting. Your brother and sister-in-law, your father and mother, and about ten others who you barely recognize wait on this dark chunk of leftover moon rock. While under the glass dome you are all protected from the emptiness and depth of space. Everyone is in shock. You can see the Earth and watch it start to crumble and implode. You feel everyone's fear. You are frightened by the idea of trying to make a 'life' under the dome. The lack of skill and supplies to survive is apparent. You feel intense fear. You look around the dome out into space, and it is nothing but darkness. You are in the darkest point of the universe and understand that you will never be able to escape.

Many under the dome begin to argue while trying to figure out the best idea for survival. You realize there is no such reality as survival at this point. You accept your fate to die. Suddenly, all of you feel a massive shake to the ground of the dismantled moon. You look up and see the dome wobbling and rocking back and forth. As you peer out toward the Earth, all of you watch its final implosion into nothingness. It is as if all the gravity pressed and compressed the Earth into dust. All of you weep as you lose your loved ones, homes and hopes for living the life you once did. You cannot help but feel helpless and scared in the darkness of space with no Earth to call home. You look around at the fiery side of the moon and see it pulled out of orbit. You scream to everyone, "This is it"!

Everyone looks over in fear as they see the burning side of the moon floating toward the dome. Now, it is as if there are two moons. You see the flaming portion of the remaining rock come closer and closer but, suddenly it drops below the star horizon and breaks off. After the break of the burning side of the moon, the other half begins to float away with all of you on it. You all know and accept your soon to come deaths as you drift out far into space. You look around, you are scared, you feel the cold, and stare into the continuous spin. You look up and see the dome begin to shake and crack from the freezing temperature and constant pressure.

You look around to speak to your brother and sister-in-law but, they have frozen in time. You become overwhelmed and motion to your father and mother but, they are also frozen solid without a trace of life. You look to the ten people and, as you try to speak, you see them freeze solid one after the other. You are terrified as you are the only one left under the cracked dome in the middle of outer space. You panic about being all alone in the depths and darkness of space and time. Everything grows darker as you remain the last one alive. And now, it's just another memory.

JUMP & FLY

Jump & Fly

You are flying. You know all you must do is jump off the ground and fly around. You bring the wind to you. You call it and energize it through your mind and with your arms. You are competing on the streets of Pass Avenue and, it is growing quite dark. There are two different curbs filled with people at the competition. You know you are competing to be the best flier. You will jump up off the ground and soar through the air. The more in tune your emotions become, the further you fly into the air. The more empowered you feel, the broader the distance you can travel. The grander your feelings, the higher you are lifted. You conjure the wind to flow up through your body and carry you outward toward the sky. As you compete, you become more confident in your skills. You know you are jumping the highest. You know you are the best at the takeoff and hovering in the air ever so swiftly. You feel so powerful and talented.

A few other competitors are flying in the air with you. You see them soaring below you. You feel their ambition and your chance to be the best you can be. You watch them fly and, they can't get as high into the air as you. You recognize there is no competition because of your astonishing flying skills. You are confidently arrogant and arrogantly confident in your rare ability. As you become more aware of your power, you ascend exceedingly high in the air. You take such an incredible flight that you blow away from Pass Avenue. The street where you learned to ride a bike, pick a paper tree with your brother, and obtain a memory of the silhouette cast by the sun on the old house you grew up.

You feel the hard and cold breeze against your face. Way up high, you see the Pass Avenue house again and specifically, the weeping willow tree your mother planted in the front yard when you were a child. The light and dark of dusk captures your excitement and your fear. You envision your accomplishments of earlier at the competition when you continued to jump off the ground and show your flying capabilities to the many people watching. You win the competition and, you are the best flyer. No one much thought you would be the winner for some reason or another. You must give a hand to your youngest maternal uncle who rooted for you to win by cheering extremely loud. After all, he was the only one who believed you would win.

The wind is now overwhelming, and the competition is over for you. This brings you from what you envisioned and into the reality of the end. You are at peace with this. There are so many competitors still trying to jump in the air and fly like you but, no one is achieving the heights you soar. You impress yourself with dedication. The feelings of overwhelm, excitement and empowerment rush through your body. The competitors and the observers see you as a flying master. You feel as if there is nothing you cannot do. As the wind keeps chauffeuring you further in the distance, you feel proud, reluctant, afraid, and at peace with drifting into the unknown. You can hear everyone but see no one. As you drift farther away into the dusk sky, you wonder how you will ever return to the ground. However, the wonder ceases when the positive and negative of your successful flight create a balance of thoughts and feelings beyond your need for control. And now, it's just another memory.

kissing
fish

Kissing Fish

You are at a pond that reminds you of a river and, it is dusk. You are fishing and enjoying yourself. You know your mother is there but, you cannot see her. She is off in the distance. You can hear her voice. You listen to her advice about your fishing skills. She is nothing but encouraging and connected to your every cast. You continue to feel your mother's presence. You are standing on a bunch of rocks uplifted from the pond river water. You end up catching a fish. You reel it in and respect the fish for giving its life to your nutrition. You thank the fish several times and appreciate its sacrifice for your health.

After you catch your fish, a shark appears in the water. The shark swims closer and closer to you and attempts to bite your hand off as you reach for the fishing line that was dangling into the water. The shark does not make contact or bite you but, you feel threatened. You begin to sharpen a long piece of wood into a sharp stake for stabbing. You proceed to spear the shark through the center of its chest and quickly pull the weapon from its lifeless body. The shark is now floating upside down and you know it is dead even though it is not bleeding.

You look around at the pond river stream and recognize how shallow and clear the water is. You see a bed of rocks shaped like a pillow for your head. You rest your body in the shallow river pond. It is only 3-feet deep, so you can see the bottom with much transparency. You realize how damaging the shark incident is to your ambitions for fishing. You attempt to try again but, the vibration of success and gratitude are gone. You decide not to fish anymore because the energy is imbalanced.

So, you lay down on the bed of rocks where you rest your head on the rock pillow. Your hair is floating in the water and is much longer than you remember. You feel the refreshing coolness of the water touch your skin. You hear your mother again, talking in the background. You do not know what she is saying, but her tone of voice soothes you. The surrounding nature is so peaceful, and you are filled with gratitude to be where you are. You are at peace. As you lean your head back further into the water to feel the cold rush of the river stream, you experience tugs and kisses on your scalp and hair. These nibbling kisses that you sense emulate suction cups. It surprises you so much that you smile, giggle, and laugh from being tickled. You realize that all these tiny fish are giving you greetings of affection. They continue to kiss and pull at your hair.

You can hear their little nibbles and suctions directly into your ears and this time, instead of giggling, it makes you laugh super hard. You smile and laugh as you receive so much love from so many little fish. You feel their mini fish teeth graze your scalp and you become serene. You are in disbelief about their tenderness as they continue to send positivity. They communicate gratitude through their endearment. They telepathically thank you for killing the shark who eats their ancestral line. You encourage their future offspring. You feel appreciated and respected. And now, it's just another memory.

love.
thine.
self.

Love. Thine. Self.

You are on a trip and traveling to another country. You visit some sites and look out upon waterfalls, cliffs, historical buildings, and a grand atmosphere of environmental beauty. You are on a giant bluff that is filled with rock formations and behind you is a hotel equipped with a restaurant. Your mother is there in the distance. You can see she is helping people check the edge of the waterfall to ensure it is safe. Swiftly, your mother transforms into a different friend of yours from elementary school. She is dressed in shorts, flip-flop sandals, and a black backpack which is a distinct part of her identity. While you watch nature and your mother's transformation, you are aware that you have stuffed an extensive ribbon-shaped and, napkin-like substance that tastes like a cigarette down your throat.

You do this for what appears as no apparent reason but, understand it is a necessary action. The napkin is so long that it far past your throat and stomach. You know it doesn't belong in your body and, you start to pull the startling paper-like substance out of your mouth. You continue to yank yards and yards of this material from your throat. The paper is so long you feel it will never end. You gag, choke, and it pauses your breathing. You gain the confidence through your disgust to keep pulling. It is nasty and, you feel filthy from the process, but you keep extracting to free yourself. The relentlessness of the countless feet of paper within you continues to surge.

Finally, you recognize there is a humungous pile of wet and white paper all over the ground next to you as you stand by a stairwell. It is complete. It is all out of you. You are oddly unafraid and at ease with the fact that this happened. You handle the problem with grace and little fear. Suddenly, you see a concerned cleaning lady and, she asks if you are alright. "Are you alright, Miss"? You understand that she knows you are okay and is simply being polite. You feel bad and apologize for your mess. "I am so sorry about the mess I made," you say with a sincere voice. She is understanding and reassures you with her eyes and body language that a cleaning lady with integrity never minds picking up after anyone.

Now that you feel much better, you make your way up the cement stairway. You see your mother again at a distance. What was once your mother transformed, is now your mother again. You feel strange about the transition but, not in the moment. The historical site covered in artistry, the sounds of the waterfall, and the clarity of the mountains take your mind to definitively divine thoughts. You feel at peace in the environment. Your mother checks on the waterfall again and you watch her as you become afraid for her balance. She is alright though, as she gracefully moves from left to right on the natural rocky cliff. You are 100-feet away, admiring your mothers' finesse, and the intensity of your surroundings.

You and your mother telepathically decide to meet at the restaurant. The historic building is breathtaking. You see your mom appear next to you and smile. You stand together in a hallway waiting to take your seats. You look down at your arms and notice you are holding four females. One, a tiny baby that fits into the palm of your hand and another a medium sized infant on your right arm. You also see an average sized one-year-old and, a little adult lady in your arms. You love all four of them so much and, you know they need help to be seated. So, you carry all four of them to their table. You slowly and carefully set each of them down one at a time. As you release them, there is a man sitting in the booth and, he has one of your belongings.

The strange man looks up at you with his little grey mustache while smoking profusely. The ashtray is overflowing. He reaches out and hands you your green-cylindrical cigarette container. He immediately gives your belonging back to you because he didn't know it was yours. You take it with reluctance because you do not smoke anymore. Suddenly, you notice another man in the booth who is waiting to see what you will do. You quickly ignore him and focus on how much you love and adore the four lovely ladies you carried to the table. You love them so much and do not want to leave them. However, even though you do not want to part them, you muster the courage to say goodbye. You go and let them eat their dinner. You know your mother is waiting for you at the front of the restaurant anyhow.

As you walk toward your mother, you look down and are carrying yourself in your arms. It is you. It is you in your arms. You are a baby. You are holding yourself so near. You cannot believe you are carrying yourself. You are overtaken by joy and disbelief. You are two months old in your 34-year-old self's arms. You look up and see that your mother is not waiting in the hallway but is making motions to sit at another table. You look down at your arms again and see that you are about a year old now. Your mother motions to you to sit down. You sit in the booth and admire yourself as a baby in a bucket car seat. "Look at me, I look so cute and, I am so big! Can you even believe this?" You hug and kiss your baby-self. Your mother looks at you and says, "You are doing such an excellent job as a mother!" In your mind, you know you are not a mother to yourself but, you are thankful for your mother's compliment.

You didn't take notice before but, you see your maternal aunt's friend across the table from you. Not your friend from your elementary school but, your aunt's friend from High School. Two old friends now mothers who swept into your life at a simultaneous time, now forgotten. You are surprised to see her because it has been too long. You greet her and, all of you begin to eat.

Your maternal aunt's friend asks, "Who is this you have here?" You reply with, "Hey, meet me from the past!" You and her laugh and gasp for air in disbelief. She responds with, "Oh my god, no way is that possible!"

As you begin to eat, you put your infant-self on your lap. You give a big hug to the sweet baby whose eyes are your own. You touch your soft baby skin. You put yourself back in your hi-chair and begin to feed yourself. You are a messy baby and, you are getting food everywhere. Your adult-self doesn't care and, you generously and gratefully clean yourself up. You are on the inner side of the booth and feel very safe. Your mother and maternal aunts' friend are sitting with you while eating, smiling, and enjoying you take care of who you are. Your baby self is to the left of you, happy as can be and gently starting to fall asleep. You enjoy the dinner and the company. You nurture the pure love and joy. You feel the overwhelm of the moment and happiness springs tears from your eyes. And now, it's just another memory.

SNOW
MOUNTAIN
LOVE

Snow Mountain Love

You are with your love at a ski resort and, it is quite cold outside. The weather is dark but, bright as if a storm and a sunset just collided in the sky. There is a cabin at the top of the snowy mountain and both of you can see the ski resort through your loving eyes. The resort is available to anyone who manages to discover it. You know that you can stay as long as you want. You know that everyone who works or is staying there will welcome you with open arms. It is a community, and everyone works together. You know there is plenty of space to relax at the resorts lounge. It is on the upper deck, has plenty of fluffy pillows, and is filled with soft-oversized comfortable chairs. As you look around, cozy fireplaces roar with gleam so bright, the light reflects off the face of your love. Your love looks so attractive and glowing from the flickering beams. You know how happy you are. You feel nothing but gratitude and excitement about the night ahead.

You and your love go inside the resort room to get dressed. You bundle up in all your ski clothing. You are both ready for the winter outdoors. You head outside. You and your love are so happy. You both feel the excitement of the new adventure. You feel the thrill of being in the snow and playing together. You and your love look at each other all bundled up and slide down a gigantic snow-covered hill. You yell "Yaaahhhoooo"! And "Yeehaw"! across from one another as you glide down the mountain. You both love every second of it. The happiness and enchantment are overwhelmingly joyous. You feel gratitude toward snow gliding with your true love. It is beyond cool. You both laugh so hard as you make silly faces and get hit with bits of snow while barreling down the mountain. You joke, play, and act like little penguins on your bellies and backs. Your inner children and adult selves play to unify. You kiss. It is beautiful and, it is pure.

You go up and down the summit six times together. Each time, you both get a little further and a little faster. You push yourselves closer and closer to the edge of the mountain for the thrill of it. You continue to feel enveloped with enjoyment. You cannot wait to repeat your delight. The second time you both are a little frightened by the speed going down the slick snowy mountain but, it quickly passes and, you both laugh and rejoice victoriously with another kiss. You both know that the little bit of fear you experience is where the excitement lives. You feel the enlightenment of being afraid and know it will better serve you both.

The third time, you feel like you are going to fall off the side of the mountain because of how fast you are going but the feeling passes shortly and, you remain safe at the bottom of the hill where you kiss your love again. The fourth time down the mountain, you grab your loves hand to warm it with your hot breath. Your love pulls their hand away because they don't like it and would rather stroke your hair, put it behind your ear, and stare into your eyes. You look deep into one another. A passionate kiss follows. The kiss is loving, and the internal message of "I'm so happy to be with you" overwhelms your heart. You are eternally grateful. The fifth time happens just before the trip to the mountain mini market. You and your love are playing in the snow together on the ground. You are rolling around, kissing, and acting silly. A couple walks by. The woman is wearing a puffed purple jacket. The man is unrecognizable. Both comment on how you are kissing on the snowy floor. They look away and say, "Look how happy they are!", with disdain and sarcasm in their voices.

The sixth and last time down snow mountain love, you land in each other's arms. You look into each other's eyes again. You feel profound. You love each other so much and feel the electric energy between the two of you. There is so much admiration. You lie in the snow together and have your legs overlapped a bit. You intertwine your arms and, your love kisses you passionately again. You begin to recognize a few realities. Your love doesn't adore you because you are beautiful, even though you are. Your love doesn't admire you because you are smart, even though you are. Your love doesn't appreciate you for your kindness, even though you are kind. You are loved simply because, you are.

You are loved despite your faults and your lover makes you feel that way. You love your lover the way they deserve to be loved. Continuing to get kissed deeply, you are enchanted by your lover's warm breath and strong embrace. You once more stare into each other's eyes as you both press your warm bodies together in the crisp and cold air. You kiss over and over again. You love each other and, it shows. You kiss even deeper as you lie in the snow. You are blissful. Your heart is aligned with who you are.

Suddenly, you are under this little rectangular overhang outside of the mountain market. The market is within the resort grounds at the very bottom of the snowy mountain where you and your love had a blast sliding down. It is in a perfect spot, really. You and your love cannot stop kissing and rolling on the ground in the snow. You are all over one another, repeatedly playing with each other and, you both love it. The life you are living feels like a holiday. You begin to get cold so, you both walk toward the mini market. After the sixth glide down, you both decide it is time to warm your bones by the fireplace inside. The market is awesomely equipped with snacks and hot beverages. It is a quaint little sanctuary from the briskness of the outdoors.

You see that there is a teenage boy whose father owns the place. You do not know him but, he speaks to you and your love about how his father came to acquire the location. He also mentions how picky your love is about hot beverages and how the demand for quality hot coffees and cocoas requires specific flavor standards which are of great value to your love. You and your love start laughing. You both are cracking up that the kid is only about fourteen years old, running his dad's shop, and making quite a vocal observation about your love's beverage preferences. The kid is so sweet and kind, you oddly but protectively continue to remind yourself that you never met him before.

You and your love are so peaceful from the warmth of the fire, soothing hot drinks, kindness from the boy, and a full day of activities that brought laughter and joy. You drink your drinks with large smiles and head outside the market doors hand in hand. You feel at peace on the adventure at snow mountain with your love. And now, it's just another memory.

SPIRIT
CAVE

Spirit Cave

You are in a deep cavern. You are unsure where the dystopian grotto is, but the resemblance of a cave is apparent. The cave made of only trash. The trash is piled up all around the edges of the cavern and, it is as if the cave emerges out of the garbage. The walls look like pressed flowers in a book but only detritus replaces the beauty of what flowers could have been. Suddenly, a Native American woman appears and begins speaking to you about how to love. She fades in and out of your vision while you are inside the trash carved cave but, you feel her presence and message of endearment.

You stand up and feel hazy from all the whispering words she utters. You know what you must do, and you are willing to do it with love. You see your first significant love out of the dusty rubbish filled setting. Your old love looks at you with a profound and entranced glare while standing on a heap of trash. Eyes glow within the cave instilling intrigue and fear. The Native American woman mutters a few more words while disappearing and reappearing in a smoke-like formation.

You walk through the trash heap cave and fall through a steep hole. The depth of the fall is forgotten the moment you hit the ground, and, at the bottom, you experience a resounding thought in your mind. You think to yourself, "It's easier to get to Earth from Hell rather than Heaven and, that is why it is so hard to fight temptations here." You rethink, "What does that even mean"? And, "What am I doing"?

You are now at the bottom of the cave, sitting on a vined throne while you sleep. The throne has all types of plant life interweaved to make it appear like a holy and hierarchical chair. You dream as you rest on the throne. You scream in your dream and, you feel fear as you sleep. You yell louder and louder. You exclaim so vibrantly that you wake yourself from your dream. You find yourself in a large room sitting on the plant throne where your shaded ex-lover gathered numerous people to demonstrate torture upon you.

Your shaded-ex lover is evil, a demon; trying to kill you. This lover is very different from your first significant love. Everyone surrounding your shaded ex-lover is thirsty to kill you. They all want to watch you suffer and ultimately die. They scream at you. Scare you. Poke you and torture your soul from the inside out. They tease and torment you with the idea of death and how you are going to die. They implant images in your mind as they circle to hurt you. They show how extinction will come for you and how death will swallow you whole. They reveal how the end will demolish your very being and sacrifice your happy memories.

From the torture, you scream at all of them. You shout at your shaded ex-lover and repeatedly exclaim, "Who are you! Who are you"! You know you will never forgive the ex-devil for this cruelty. Never. They are dead in your heart and, all the fear of evil surrounding the extracted love has vanished. "Let me have it then"! you bellow. "Get this over with if you are going to do it"! You see a new vision where the actual devil is the last to show its face. The demon mentally stalks you with swords, stakes, and conjures eviler.

All the demonic cronies surround you with their weapons and, as they come forward one by one with the devil at their side, you feel each sword and stake drive through your body. You sense every inch of the blades piercing your guts and draining your core. You repeatedly endure the negative feelings, energies, and physical atrocities without fear. As you undergo the terror and the pain from each sharp edge dissolving your bodies lifeforce, you fade into darkness but, only to rejuvenate from your disposal.

Rapidly, you sit at a freshly painted white table. The table is so bright it is challenging to see clearly. A small dove is perched at the table and, you look at it with intention and utter gratitude for its beauty and calming presence. You recognize a note placed next to the dove and, it fills you with admiration. The message is on a white note card and written with what appears to be golden ink. However, the message reads blank and disappears from memory. Luckily, it instills feelings of hope, faith, and belief. You believe in yourself while sitting at the white table and believe in the universe while staring at the dove. You feel cloaked in epiphany. You are radiated by pain and sacrifice. And now, it's just another memory.

THREE
BIRTHS

Three Births

You are in a land of avalanches, tundra, and frozen winds. The world is dormant, desolate, and this is the Earth you know in this time and space. There is a snowmobile master. He looks like someone familiar but not physically, only mentally; but only semi-mentally, mostly perceptually. You have a history with him. You know there is love but, you do not like him much. You think he is egoistic, a show-off, and short-sighted in his thinking. You know it is not precisely him but, all the attributes are there that you couldn't care less. Regardless, he is there with you.

Despite his fleeting presence, you are confused and, you are alone. You are running and freezing until you reach a summit with an apartment. When you arrive at the complex your, mother is there. You are so cold and feel like you are turning blue. The world is so different now and, you are unsure what you need to do next. Other family and friends are there but, you do not know who they are. The world is not the same as it once was to you.

You start to feel pain throughout your body. The painfulness is unrecognizable. You look at the walls around you and, they begin to shake. The walls continue to rattle in a commiserating response to your pain. You look down and see that you are bleeding profusely all over the floor. The pain increases times ten and so does the rattling of the walls. There is so much bright red blood. The sight of your bleeding quickly makes you panic. You are terrified. You do not know what to do.

Your mother hurries you to a circular restroom with a high ceiling shower made of octagonal glass and, there is an adjacent much longer plate of glass you cannot see through. It looks a lot like detective's glass when they question and identify criminals. You feel there is more to this room than there seems but, you are uncertain as to what it could be. The pain inside your body increases as you lay on a steel table bleeding horrifically. You think you may pass out from all the pain and blood but, you manage to stay awake. You are bearing down in pain. The most intense agony you have ever felt strikes through your abdomen. Then, the excruciating torture spreads throughout your entire body.

Blood is now all over the steel table, the high ceiling shower, and the plate glass window. Your mother is right there with you. She helps you every step of the way. She is supportive. She is giving. She is encouraging. She continues to motivate and inspire you. You finally become aware of your extra-large belly and recognize you are not ordinarily pregnant but, incredibly pregnant. You are humungous. The bleeding is not stopping. As you continue to hemorrhage excessive quantities of blood, you are scared and, you consider your mother's eyes who only speak with compassion for your pain and fear. You feel your mother's vulnerability and despite her shocking voice and statements, "You are giant"! and "It is time"! you trust her judgement.

Your mother tells you to push. You push hard and, more blood gets all over the octagonal room and plate glass. The steel table is cold and stained with scarlet red. You thrust hard and out comes a giant baby, much more massive than any realistic newborn could ever possibly be. The baby's back is towards you and you never see its face. Your mother screams, "It's a girl"! Happiness ensues in the room. Your baby gets wrapped up somehow and whisked off to safety. You know a frozen world is not safe for newborn babies so, you, let your baby go. You are still profusely bleeding, and the walls remain covered in splatters of blood. You feel the physical and mental anguish of your baby swept off to the unknown.

You are confused about why you are still bleeding so badly. You have already delivered so why are you still in pain? Your mother is there by your side. She tells you the next baby is coming. You think to yourself, "Another baby is coming"! You are overwhelmed that there is another baby inside you. You look at your mother alarmingly. You hold her hand tightly as she encourages you once more. Your mother helps and reaches down to pull out your baby this time so, it will be less difficult for you. Your mother screams again in shock and joy, "It's a girl"! She hands your baby girl to you and, you swaddle her in your right arm but, your baby is looking away and you can only see a poorly lit side profile. Another baby will not survive in this world of frozen disaster so, your daughter is wrapped up somehow and whisked off to safety.

You are relieved from pain at the end of the deliveries but feel empty about your two babies that you may never see again. You mention to your mother, "I feel like this is not over, mom." You experience a movement that makes you feel there is something else. Your mother checks your belly, presses on your abdomen, and says, "You have another baby inside you"! "Oh, my god, a third, it's triplets"! Your last baby doesn't even need a push and, comes flying out of you like a force of gravity pulling from the inside out. Your mother screams one more time with a, "It's a girl"! You never see your third baby's face because as it flies from the womb, it hits the plate glass window, and disappears into swaddled safety. However odd the occurrence, this time you know you will see all your babies again.

You remain in your gory hospital nightgown with the memories of your three babies. The urgency of meeting back up with your infant's fuels your desire to heal and survive. Your mother is now gone, and you know you must run. You realize that you are out of the octagonal glass room and back in the freezing tundra with your old friend Johnnie. You link arm in arm as you begin to run. You feel and see the snow beneath your feet. You discern the frost overtaking your body. You hear the crashing of ice and splitting of the ground under you. You and Johnnie yell out safety directions and glide as you run together. With your arms linked you become an extension of one another. You both glance behind and recognize you are running from a tumbling and fast-moving avalanche.

You both make turns and strides in unison at every possible moment to avoid shards of ice and icicles cutting you both like glass. You run and jump together with the decisiveness to make full-on Olympian leaps over groundbreaking beneath you while landslides fall. Johnnie supports your weight and encourages your strength as you continue to bleed onto the white snow now turned the color red. Johnnie sees your suffering, feels your pain, and is determined to help you to safety. You run with Johnnie and your hospital gown blows in the frost pierced wind while the trail of painful disaster is left behind.

You arrive at an open and icy field surrounded by close and significantly tall mountains. You are still linked arm in arm with Johnnie who wants to inspire your courage. Johnnie needs you both to make it to the icy shore where the snowmobile master is waiting for everyone. As you recognize your bleeding again, worries for your life begin to fester. A small group of five people wait and anticipate the arrival of the snowmobile master. Already having given birth to the three babies and running for your life through the tundra, you are exhausted, still losing blood, and in so much pain. You shake from the shocking cold and series of traumatic events. Luckily, you make it to shore in time to meet the master.

You watch across the open icy field as multiple avalanches break the frozen ocean water and impede your chances of escaping the shore. Time is crucial and, snow begins to fall. The snowmobile master arrives and scoops up the five people waiting. You and Johnnie feel the shock from the master leaving you both in such a condition. You both hope he will come back to save you. A moment later, he returns just in time but, not for you. You do not understand what happens. The snowmobile master left without you while simultaneously, Johnnie disappears. You are angry. You are hurt. You are terrified. You are alone and left to freeze, bleed, and die without a trace of seeing your babies ever again. Although somehow, it is not over, and you suddenly end up back where you began.

In pain and still bleeding, you are next to the octagonal room and, in opposition to the plate glass where you gave birth to your three babies. You can see into the octagonal room. As you peer in, it is sparkling clean. There is no evidence of your births and, there is no sign of your three infants. When you were in the octagonal room laying on the steel table before giving birth, you could not see what was behind the glass but, now on the other side, you can see everything. You turn from inspecting the room and view a fire pit ablaze in the center of a circular lecture hall.

An unknown male professor gives a lecture and virtual presentation on a 3D projector. You see your brother and, you haven't seen him in a very long time. He is listening to the professor speak while taking notes amongst very few students. He is busy and studying diligently. He gazes up from his focus on his written notes every so often to look at the presentation and the professor lecturing. The circular hall and brick walls overwhelm your senses and, you look up to see an open roof to the stars. The sky is majestic and, like nothing you have ever seen. It is gorgeous and remarkably intense. You can see the Milky Way and trillions of star lights that glow and sparkle into your eyes. You attempt to walk over to your brother because you are excited to see him but, you are slow to reach him. He does not see or hear you. He is studying so intently with paper notes and a laptop.

You are still in extreme pain and drag your broken and bleeding body in his direction. You are wearing the blood stain hospital gown. You call to get his attention by waving and speaking his name. Through a corridor while gazing up at the lecture hall seats, you almost make it to him. You see the look on his face and, you feel his overwhelming unhappiness, but admire his demonstration of the diligence necessary to succeed. You sense the rough cold and pain come over you as you bleed, wait, and hope. Your brother finally looks up. He sees you. Both your eyes meet. You mouth your thoughts but, no voice comes out. You ask for his help. He shows you that he feels your torment and discomfort as he reaches out to grab your arm. Before he connects, you remember your three babies and how you will never see them again. You begin to sob. And now, it's just another memory.

TURTLE
GARDEN

Turtle Garden

Here you are. You have never been here before. Surrounding you is a backyard resembling a greenhouse and garden. There are bushes, shrubs, flowers, waterfalls, and an 8ft.-white fence encompassing the property in the shape of a square. You look at all the many colors of the flowers and breathe in the fresh plant-cleansed air. Everything is green and full of life. You are impressed and excited but also, feel scared and awkward. You know that for some reason, you cannot leave but, you are unsure why. You are unquestionably stuck. You know there is a house upfront even though you thought you had never been there before. You also know multitudes of people are traveling in the front house, so you don't go back. You see a glass sliding door to an outside garden but, run into your father briefly who chats for a time and then leaves. You are unsure what your father says but, you know it was nothing pertinent.

The backyard garden is quite magnificent. There are the grandest trees and ponds at your every glance and small waterfalls lining each corner of the greenhouse-shaped structure. Fountains, decadence, and unending foliage encompass your vision. It is glorious. It is pristine. It is stupendous but, at the same time, you feel frightened and you do not know why. You are engrossed in the backyard garden and recently given a small turtle to take care of and protect. The man who gave you the turtle lives up in the front house and, this was why you do not want to go back inside. However, the turtle given to you is very young, small, and super cool. You love the turtle.

You carry the little turtle in your hands and plan to take him with you when you leave because you consider it your responsibility. With the turtle in your hands, you look around the grandiose backyard and spot a fountain. You notice a giant stone tortoise on its hind legs with translucent-flowing water pouring into a circular basin filled with a variety of lily pads. The fountain has green and white lights shining onto it to accentuate its elegant design. You recognize its beauty. The tortoise is greyish green with purposeful wrinkles of wisdom all over its body. It also has distinct parallelogram shell indentations. The tortoise statue is well-crafted and true to life size. You consider it quite impressive.

The little turtle is still in your hands as you gaze at the giant tortoise statue. The water continues to flow into the circular basin where all the lily pads sway back and forth. You glance at the sweet little turtle in your hands and gaze at the water in the basin. You notice the turtle is becoming fidgety and giving you signs it wants to jump in the water. Then, you start to feel the turtle is unhappy in your hands and wants you to let it go onto the lily pads. You feel apprehensive, but you know you love the turtle enough to free it. So, you let the turtle leap from your hands and swim around in the fountain. You watch as it repeatedly glides on top of the water and, around the lily pads. You see and feel the turtle's happiness. You know you did the right thing. You look around again at the majestic yard and think of how breathtaking it all is. You breathe in the scents of the greenery, herbs, and sweet roses stinging the air with perfume.

You look back at the fountain to check on the swimming turtle. You see the little reptile safe and chugging through the fountain water. It is then that you notice the tortoise statue start to turn its head. You are uncertain if it is real but, feel intense fear. Its eyes open wide and look deeply at you. The tortoise is alive, and you are terrified. The creature mumbles and moves each limb a little more with each passing second. You are scared, in shock, and unsure what to do as you slowly back away. You see its giant legs and shell start shifting into a different stance. Its massive head is covered in plate-like fins that resemble prehistoric-armor.

Then, the tortoise begins to speak to you in a taunting and demeaning manner. Once you hear it speak, you run to the back of the yard in extreme fear. It continues to speak to you. It sends low and negative tones of voice that you cannot distinctly understand. You are scared and hide in the depths of the backyard. As you hide, you hear a house next door having a party. You are unsure what home in the neighborhood is hosting. You finally assume it is not a neighbor at all and that it must be the guy from the front house who gave you the turtle. Amidst your distraction, the tortoise speaks to you more clearly. In low and vibrating negative tones, the tortoise aggressively expresses, "I do not like anything human or anyone in my garden! Do not even think or attempt to take the baby turtle with you if you ever manage to leave"!

The tortoise shifts its giant shell and surprisingly fast-moving body through the garden to hunt you. It gets up on its hind legs and chases you through the beautiful plant-life. You run, jump, and hide to escape its unrelenting search. It is hard for you to get away from its speedy movements and intellectual decisions. You attempt to flee the trap by walking across a concrete wall. Panicking and scared you trudge the 8-foot divider. You look down and see that the yard next door contains thorns capable of killing you if you fall. You take your chances walking the wall while knowing there are only three possible outcomes. One, you may survive, two, you may fall over to the neighbors' thorny backyard and die, or three, the tortoise may catch you and then, you perish anyway. Whatever the outcome, escape is worth the risk.

You continue to walk the wall. You get a quarter of the way to freedom and realize how visible you are. You drop down and hang from your hands to hide. You are on the neighbor's side of the wall and feel the concrete pressing into your palms. You hear the tortoise chasing your hands as you dangle and quickly grab to get to the front of the garden. You grip so tightly it leaves marks and, your hands start to bleed. You dangle and grab the wall repeatedly as you move swiftly to escape. You feel like everything is going in slow motion. You feel the pressure of your body pulling more on your hands as you suspend in air. You hear the tortoise making loud grumbling sounds and yelping more negative tones. You know that it wants you to leave but only after it catches and has its way with you.

You cannot hold on much longer as the concrete wall digs deeper into your bloody hands. You stop and rest for a moment while viewing the neighbor's backyard of thorns. The majesty of the garden is lost, and you feel no joy. You only feel pain, suffering, fear, and the desperateness to survive. You hear the tortoise find you. You pose like a stiff board in hopes of going unseen. Unfortunately, and quickly, the tortoise peaks its head through a hole in the concrete wall. Its stare is infinitely frightening and makes your heart race. Its gaze exhausts your spirit with its glowing green and blue eyes.

It distinguishes you and utters negative words about the endangerment of its species. It sends you non-verbal messages that the fear you feel is the fear it has felt every waking day of its life. The tortoise is a dictator, instilling psychological fear and physical ridicule. It angerly stares at you through the hole in the wall. The tortoise is furious with humanity. It has a severe wound in its heart and in its ancestry, that you empathetically feel. It begins to speak and says, "My babies have been stolen for decades by people just like you! I will not let this ever happen again no matter how many babies the man in the house disposes"! You understand the rage and undeniable pain. You express to the creature as you stare into its bright and terrifying eyes through the hole in the concrete, "I am not one of those people and I am going to leave your garden. I am not taking your baby, and I will never come back again"!

The tortoise responds to your suggestion by staring at you and lunging to initiate a deadly race to drive you out of the garden. The creepy and inquisitively negative vocal tones resonate in your mind as you hurriedly scale the wall to freedom. You see the tortoise gain on you. You know if you can get to the glass sliding door, you are safe. As you dash to the door, you understand the marathon is sabotage and, the tortoise wants to keep you trapped. It wants you to be faulty in your thinking. All along, its plan is to catch and harm you. You rush and use all your force to launch your body from the wall and toward the doorway. You make it just in time and arrive behind the glass unharmed. As the door closes behind you, you look out and see numerous other baby turtles throughout the garden. From the glass, you view the several pathways and ponds leading to and from the trees and flower patches. You see the running water from the fountains. You feel the relief and serenity of not being in the garden. It is beautiful because it is at a distance. It is now clear to you that the man in the front house did not own the enchanted, gorgeous, and terrifying garden, the reptiles did.

As you walk in the house from the back door, you finally meet the man who owns the front. He is tall, lanky, balding and has a strange resemblance to an ex-partner who abused you. You are not happy with meeting him. You think he is uncordial and in denial about the garden. He is there cooking and eating something in the kitchen that smells rotten. The kitchen is dingy, dirty, greasy, and has a window overlooking the garden and greenhouse. You tell him, "I do not want the turtle anymore since the yard is haunted…and by the way, you didn't tell me about the tortoise fountain-statue that comes to life"! The man aggressively responds with, "Do you think I care about you taking the turtle or not? Also, there is no real-life tortoise, and I am only living here for now"!? Then, he reaches for a beer from the refrigerator and cracks it open.

The man shows how much he doesn't care by continuing to cook and ignore you. You cannot seem to get your thoughts out in words. You use hand gestures to explain but he does not acknowledge you. He is totally unaware and oblivious to your garden experience that was both enchanting and terrifying. Since he pays no attention, you look out the window of the kitchen in shock to see the tortoise back in place as the fountain-statue. It is positioned just like you first saw it, immobile and uncommunicative. Now, it appears the tortoise is an illusion and the man may be correct but, you feel confident that you know what is real from what you experienced. As the statue's shell shines false beauty, you are forever reminded of what really happened in the turtle garden. And now, it's just another memory.

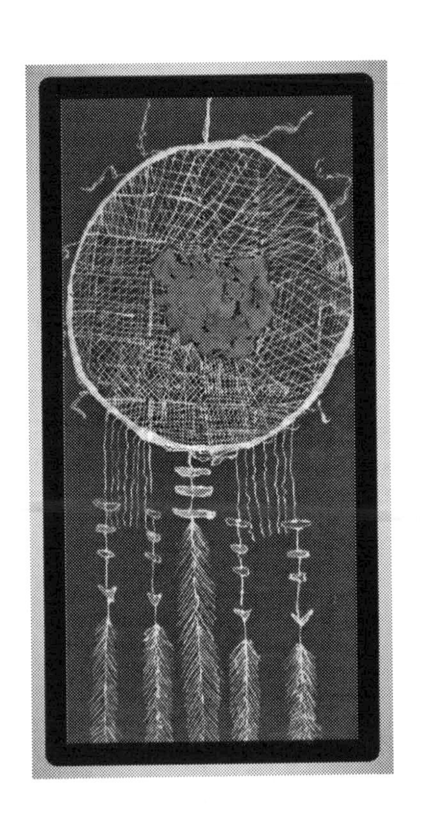

Message From The Author

Kristen Andersen, Ed. D

So, what are dreams? Are they wish fulfillment, divine message, relief from repression or a connection to the conscious? Perhaps they are a result of life experiences, a coping mechanism for pain, heightened awareness or just a physical result of sleep? Maybe dreams are nothing. While the uncertainty of the dream world will continue to perplex our minds with no definitive answers, our personal interpretation will remain reliable and up to the dreamer. Be true to yourself and the real meaning behind your dreams.

Your time is extremely valuable, and I appreciate you. Thank you for reading these dreams that are now, my unconscious memories.

Never Ending Appreciation,
Kristen Andersen, Ed. D

Quotes From Freud

"We are not in general in a position to interpret another person's dream unless he is prepared to communicate to us the unconscious thoughts that lie behind its content...We have seen that, as a general rule each person is at liberty to construct his dream work according to his individual peculiarities and so to make it unintelligible to other people. It now appears that in complete contrast to this, there are a certain number of dreams which almost everyone has dreamt alike and which we are accustomed to assume must have the same meaning for everyone...If we attempt to interpret a typical dream, the dreamer fails as a rule to produce the associations which would in other cases have led us to understand it, or else his associations

become obscure and insufficient so that we cannot solve our problem with their help…Dreams are the highway to the unconscious, often bringing to light what is in all the mental processes, especially what is deep within the Id and unconscious, in the form of dreams that play out and relieve us of what's repressed. It is often affected an individual's life circumstances, past experiences, and upbringing…The interpretation of dreams is the royal road to knowledge of the unconscious activities of the mind."
Reference
Freud, S. (1998). *The Interpretation of Dreams: Freud's Seminal Work in Understanding the Human Mind.* U.S.A: HarperCollins.

Printed in the United States
By Bookmasters